ICONIC DESIGNS

GREAT
ELECTRONIC GADGET
DESIGNS

1900-TODAY

Ian Graham

raintree

a Capstone company — publishers for children

Raintree is an imprint of Capstone Global Library Limited, a company incorporated in England and Wales having its registered office at 7 Pilgrim Street London, EC4V 6LB – Registered company number: 6695582

www.raintree.co.uk
myorders@raintree.co.uk

Edited by Clare Lewis and Abby Colich
Designed by Richard Parker
Original illustrations © Capstone Global Library Ltd 2015
Illustrated by HL Studios
Picture research by Jo Miller
Production by Victoria Fitzgerald
Originated by Capstone Global Library Ltd
Printed and bound in China by Leo Paper Products

ISBN 978 1 406 29671 6
19 18 17 16 15
10 9 8 7 6 5 4 3 2 1

British Library Cataloguing in Publication Data
A full catalogue record for this book is available from the British Library.

Acknowledgements
We would like to thank the following for permission to reproduce photographs: Alamy: Art Directors & TRIP/Helene Rogers, 32, charlie stroke, 29, Chris Wilson, 19, INTERFOTO, 21; AP Images, 8; Bloomberg via Getty Images: Tim Boyle, 39; Corbis: Sygma/Yves Forestler, 28; Dreamstime: Arnau2098, cover (inset); Getty Images: AFP/Toshifumi Kitamura, 30, AFP/Yoshikazu Tsuno, 35; Glow Images: All Canada Photos/Oleksiy Maksymenko, 34; Landov: EPA, 37; Newscom: EPA/Facundo Arrizabalaga, 41, Eye Ubiquitous, 36, Ingram Publishing, cover, MBR/KRT, 31, WENN Photos/Stefan Krempl, 10, ZUMA Press/St Petersburg Times/Tampa Bay Times, 27, ZUMA Press/Veronika Lukasova, 14; Science Source: Martin Shields, 33; Shutterstock: Artit Thongchuea, 5, Ociacia, 43, padu_foto, 23, suthiphong yina, 17, Syda Productions, 42, Twin Design, 38, vipman, 13, vlabo, 4; SuperStock: Science and Society, 16; Wikimedia: Cmglee, 7, Evan-Amos, 11, 24, George Chemilevsky, 15, Groink, 12

Design Elements
Shutterstock: franco's photos, Jason Winter, URRRA

CONTENTS

Some words are shown in bold, **like this**. You can find out what they mean by looking in the glossary.

INTRODUCING ICONIC GADGETS

Can you imagine a world without mobile phones, **personal computers**, **digital** cameras or any of the other **electronic** gadgets that we have today? In the early 1900s, none of these things had been invented yet. Electronic gadgets like these are small tools, machines or toys that have **electric circuits** inside them.

Shrinking parts

The first electronic products, such as radios, were big and heavy – too heavy to carry around. If you looked inside them, you would find electronic parts called **valves** or vacuum tubes. They looked like light bulbs. They were as big as light bulbs, and they broke just as easily.

Everything changed in the 1950s when electronic equipment started getting smaller. Tiny electronic parts called **transistors** started replacing valves or tubes. Some electronic products, especially radios, could now be made small enough and light enough for people to carry around. These were the first electronic gadgets. Later, **chips** replaced transistors. Some chips the size of a postage stamp contain millions of transistors.

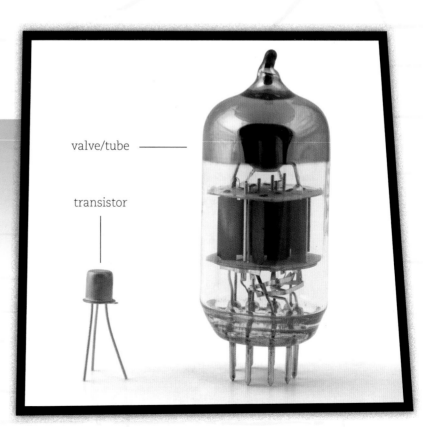

When tiny transistors replaced valves or tubes, small portable gadgets became possible.

valve/tube

transistor

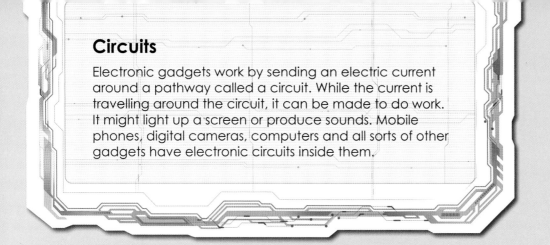

Circuits

Electronic gadgets work by sending an electric current around a pathway called a circuit. While the current is travelling around the circuit, it can be made to do work. It might light up a screen or produce sounds. Mobile phones, digital cameras, computers and all sorts of other gadgets have electronic circuits inside them.

Inside a gadget, there is a circuit board covered with chips and other parts. Metal tracks on the board connect them together, forming circuits that make the gadget work.

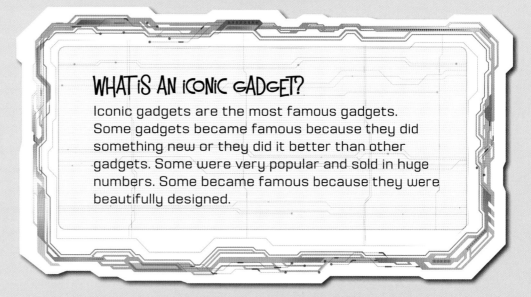

WHAT IS AN ICONIC GADGET?

Iconic gadgets are the most famous gadgets. Some gadgets became famous because they did something new or they did it better than other gadgets. Some were very popular and sold in huge numbers. Some became famous because they were beautifully designed.

REGENCY TR-1

The Regency TR-1 was the world's first transistor radio. It was the first radio that was small enough and light enough to be carried around easily. There had been portable radios before then, but they were the size of a small suitcase and very heavy. They used valves (vacuum tubes) that broke easily. The TR-1 was small enough to hold in a person's hand or slip into a pocket. It changed the way people listened to music. And it came along at exactly the right time, just as rock and roll music arrived. Teenagers wanted to listen to the music and transistor radios like the TR-1 enabled them to do it easily.

INVENTING THE TRANSISTOR

The transistor was invented by John Bardeen, Walter Brattain and William Shockley in 1947. They won one of the biggest prizes in science for their work – the Nobel Prize in Physics. They invented the transistor because they were looking for something that worked better than a valve or tube. Transistors were smaller, used less electricity and didn't break as easily.

The TR-1 had a very simple electronic circuit inside it. It used only four tiny transistors and it was powered by a small battery. Most of the other electronic parts had to be made especially for it, because small enough parts didn't exist. The radio had only two controls. One switched it on and turned up the volume. Another tuned in to different radio stations. The TR-1 let people listen to music anywhere. Its sound quality wasn't very good, but that didn't matter to people, because it was the first small, lightweight portable radio.

More than 100,000 TR-1 radios were sold. Its success led to many other **manufacturers** making their own transistor radios.

TELSTAR

FAST FACTS

Type of gadget: Communications satellite
Produced by: Bell Telephone Laboratories
Introduced in: 1962

Today, we're used to seeing live television pictures beamed into our homes from all around the world, but before the 1960s this could not be done. Telstar was the first **satellite** that could bounce live television pictures between the United States and Europe. It quickly became famous. Everybody knew the name "Telstar".

Telstar worked for only a few months, but it changed international communications forever.

STAR SATELLITE

Telstar was so famous that products and companies were named after it. Songs were even written about it. A song called "Telstar" was performed by a group called The Tornadoes. It reached number one in the music charts in several countries in 1962.

Telstar was a metal ball 88 centimetres (34 inches) across. It was sent into space on top of a rocket on 10 July 1962. Later the same month, people were amazed to see live television pictures coming from the other side of the world. The pictures could only be seen for about 18 minutes, every time the satellite flew over as it sped around the world.

Solar panels

The equipment carried by satellites uses electricity. Batteries would run out of power very quickly. Instead, satellites are powered by solar panels, which change sunlight into electricity. A back-up battery provides electricity if the solar panels turn away from the Sun or are shaded by Earth. The solar panels keep the battery fully charged.

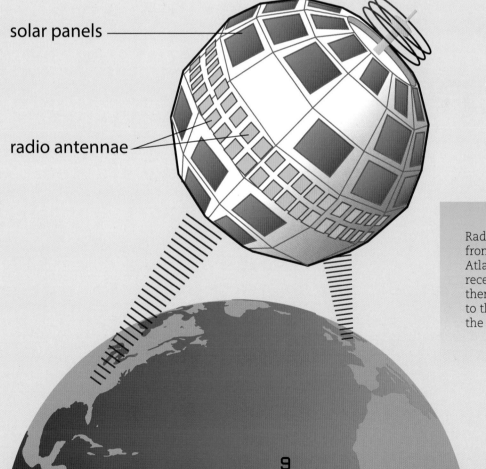

solar panels

radio antennae

Radio signals sent up from one side of the Atlantic Ocean were received by Telstar. It then sent them down to the other side of the ocean.

Ralph Baer

German-born Ralph Baer moved to the United States when he was 16. He trained as a radio service technician and then a television engineer. In 1951, he thought of making television sets that could play games, but his bosses didn't like the idea. Fifteen years later, millions of people had television sets, so he suggested making a games **console**. The games console would be a gadget that could be plugged into a TV set to play games. This time his bosses said yes.

Ralph Baer designed the games console that started the home video games industry.

Prototypes

Before a new gadget is manufactured in large numbers, one is built to make sure that everything looks right and works well. It is called a **prototype**. If any problems are found, they are put right. More prototypes might be built until the design is perfect. Then manufacturing can begin.

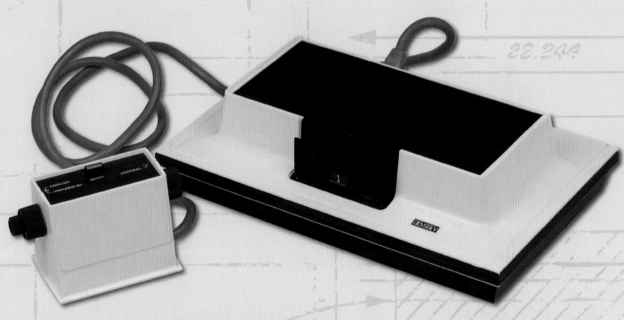

The Magnavox Odyssey was a big hit. About 130,000 were sold in the first year.

The first video game put two bright spots on a TV screen. Turning a knob on a controller made one spot chase the other spot around the screen. Another was a simple tennis game. Games were selected by plugging games cards into the console. The console was called the Magnavox Odyssey. It went on sale in 1972. It was the first-ever video games console. Baer went on to invent and design many other electronic games and gadgets.

JVC HR-3300

FAST FACTS

Type of gadget: Videocassette recorder
Produced by: JVC
Introduced in: 1976

Until the 1970s, the only people who could record television programmes were television companies. Their video tape recorders were big, hard to use and very expensive. Then in 1971, Sony made machines that recorded television programmes on a little box of **magnetic tape**. The box was called a videocassette. Videocassette recorders (VCRs) were cheaper and easier to use.

Piano key controls   Videocassette drawer

The JVC HR-3300 VCR had big clunky controls called piano keys to start recording or playing a tape.

A VHS videocassette contained up to 350 metres (1,150 feet) of video tape.

Home recording

The VCR that gave most people their first experience of home video recording was the JVC HR-3300. A videocassette was loaded into a drawer that popped up on top of the recorder.

At first, people used their VCRs to record television programmes at home. The VCR had a timer that could be set to switch the recorder on and off, but it was very easy to set the wrong time, date or television channel and record the wrong programme! Then film companies started selling videocassettes of cinema films to watch at home, too.

VIDEO WARS

The JVC HR-3300 was a type of video recorder called VHS. VHS videocassettes could be used in any VHS machine. A different type of VCR made by Sony was called Betamax. Then another company, Philips, made a third type called V2000. VHS, Betamax and V2000 videocassettes were different shapes, so they didn't fit each other's VCRs. People had to decide which type of recorder to have. VHS won the video wars.

PET

The Commodore PET was the world's first all-in-one personal computer. It was the first computer you could buy, plug in, switch on and use straight away. Everything needed was included and no more parts had to be added. Unlike most computers at that time, the PET had its own built-in screen and keyboard. It also had a tape recorder for storing **computer programs** and **data**. Its screen was a tiny 23-centimetre (9-inch) television. It looked very futuristic for its time.

PET sounds like a cuddly kitten or puppy but it actually stands for Personal Electronic Transactor.

Launching the PET

Commodore was a company that made business equipment and electronic calculators. When they saw the first home computers made by other companies, they decided to make their own computer. The result was the Commodore PET. It went on sale in 1977 and it was very successful. New improved models of the PET were made until 1986. By then it had been overtaken by other, better computers.

FLOPPY DISKS

The first home computers recorded information on magnetic tape. It worked, but it was slow. Big business computers used faster magnetic discs. They were flimsy, or floppy, so they were called **floppy disks**. Today, home computers have built-in **hard disks** that hold 10 million times more information than the first floppy disks. We now use USB Flash Drives for storing and moving data. These can be plugged into the hard drive.

The first floppy disks were 20 centimetres (8 inches) across. They were made for the big computers used by businesses. Smaller disks were made for home computers.

APPLE II

The Apple II was the first **mass-produced** personal computer. It went on sale in 1977, the same year as the Commodore PET. It was popular because it was easy to use, it worked well and it produced colour **graphics**. It also looked good compared to most other computers at that time. A lot of computers looked like a collection of boxes of electronics – something that might be used in industry or in an electronics workshop. The Apple II was designed to be a smart-looking product that could be used at home or in an office.

The Apple II computer was on sale for 16 years and about 5 million were sold.

The Apple II was designed by Steve Wozniak. He designed it so that people could plug in extra equipment made by Apple and other companies. Later, Apple replaced it with improved models that could do more and had fewer chips inside. Having fewer chips cut the cost of making the computers. Original Apple II computers were made until 1987. They were later replaced by a new Apple computer, the Macintosh.

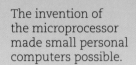
The invention of the microprocessor made small personal computers possible.

MICROPROCESSORS

Computers like the Apple II and Commodore PET were made possible by a chip called a microprocessor. It contains part of a computer called the central processing unit (CPU). The CPU carries out the instructions in a computer program and does all of the computer's calculations. Before the microprocessor, a CPU was made of hundreds of separate parts.

SONY WALKMAN

In the late 1960s and 1970s, audio tape **cassettes** were a popular way to listen to recorded music. Audio means sound. Portable cassette players were big and heavy, but the Sony Walkman changed everything. It amazed everyone who saw it, because it was so small. It wasn't much bigger than the tape cassette inside it.

It was designed because Akio Morita, one of the people who started Sony, wanted a small device for listening to music during the many long flights he had to make. The result was the Sony Walkman. Devices like the Walkman were called **personal stereos**.

DIGITAL AND ANALOGUE

There are two ways to record sound – **analogue** and digital. The first Sony Walkman used analogue recording. Sound was recorded on magnetic tape. The changing magnetic pattern on the tape matched changes in the sound. This is analogue recording. Digital recording changes sound into a series of numbers, a code that can be recorded on a tape, disc or chip. Music downloads are digital.

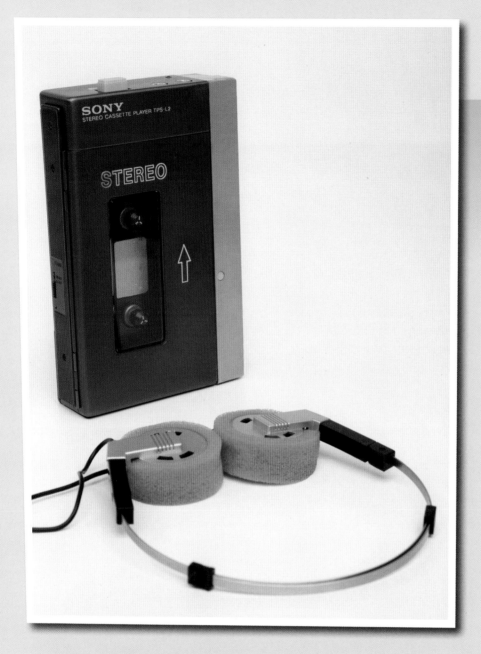

The Sony Walkman wasn't the first personal stereo, but it was the first one to be very successful all over the world.

Keeping up to date

The way people listened to music changed over the years and the Walkman changed too. The **CD** Walkman, or Discman, played compact discs (CDs) instead of tape cassettes. The Walkman MP3 had no tapes or discs inside. Instead, it stored music digitally in the same way as computers store information. Later, this type of Walkman was built into some mobile phones.

IBM PC

By 1981, there were lots of different personal computers, but they couldn't work together or "talk" to each other. A program written for one computer wouldn't run on a different computer. The IBM Personal Computer (PC) changed everything. It was designed in only 12 months. This was very fast for that time, especially for a big company like IBM. The PC was designed to make it easy to replace parts and add extra parts.

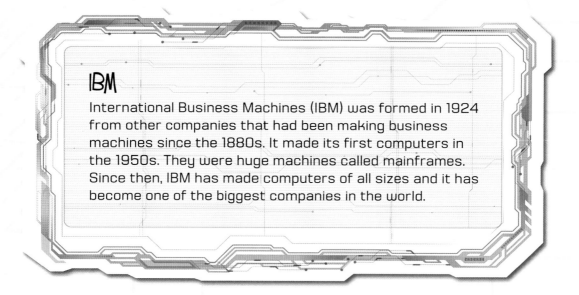

IBM

International Business Machines (IBM) was formed in 1924 from other companies that had been making business machines since the 1880s. It made its first computers in the 1950s. They were huge machines called mainframes. Since then, IBM has made computers of all sizes and it has become one of the biggest companies in the world.

The IBM PC went on sale in 1981. Until then, IBM had made only big computers for businesses, governments and universities. More than half of all of its PCs went to homes. The IBM PC was a huge success. By the end of 1982, an IBM PC was being sold somewhere every minute.

IBM was a big and important company and its PC was very successful. So, other companies started making computers that could run the same programs as the PC and use the same screens, keyboards, printers and other equipment. These other computers were called PC compatibles. Before long, they were all being called PCs.

All of today's PCs can trace their history back to the IBM PC in the 1980s.

GAME BOY

The Nintendo Game Boy was the first really successful handheld games console. It was nicknamed "the grey brick", because it was a plain grey box. Later Game Boys were made in different colours. The games played on it were sold as cartridges that players plugged into the console. Two players could play against each other by connecting their Game Boys together with a cable. A few games could be played by up to four players with their consoles connected together. The games were very simple, but they were lots of fun.

The Game Boy was designed by Gunpei Yokoi and Satoru Okada. Yokoi designed the outside and Okada designed the inside. They knew they had to keep it very simple or it would cost too much to make and the selling price would be too high.

GAMES CARTRIDGES

The Game Boy wasn't the first handheld games console to use plug-in games cartridges. The first one was called Microvision. It was produced in 1979 by Milton Bradley, an American games company. Its screen was tiny and very few games were made for it. For these reasons, it wasn't very popular.

More than 450 games
could be played
on a Game Boy by
using plug-in games
cartridges.

The Game Boy went on sale in 1989 and it was an overnight success. More than 118 million of the original Game Boys had been sold by the time manufacturing stopped in 2003. The first Game Boys were so successful that they were redesigned and improved. The new Game Boys, with different shapes and sizes, and better screens, were made until 2008.

PLAYSTATION

The Sony PlayStation was the idea of Sony executive Ken Kutaragi in the late 1980s. After a few years of research, Sony decided to go ahead with the project in 1993.

Games were to be stored on discs called CD-ROMs. CD-ROMs are the same size as music CDs, so the console would play music CDs too. At first, Nintendo and Sony worked together. The console would play Nintendo games and Sony music CDs. However, Nintendo decided not to go ahead, so Sony carried on alone.

The first PlayStation was the first games console with sales of more than 100 million.

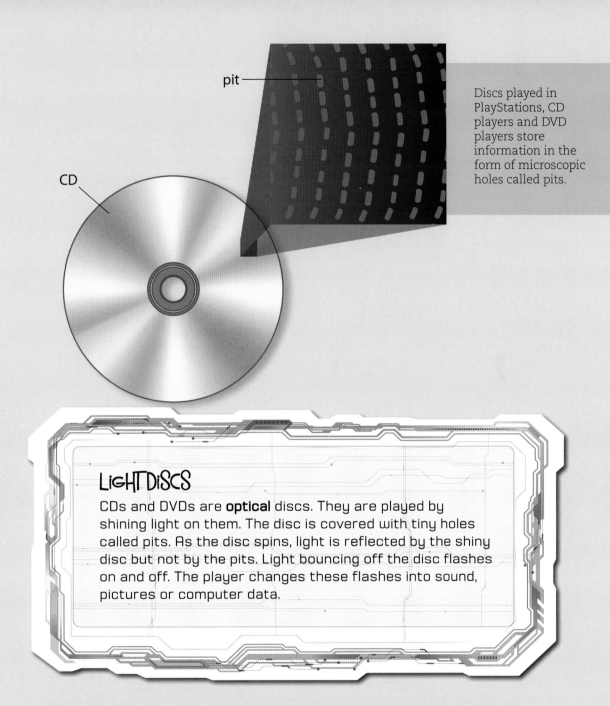

pit

CD

Discs played in PlayStations, CD players and DVD players store information in the form of microscopic holes called pits.

LiGHT DiSCS

CDs and DVDs are **optical** discs. They are played by shining light on them. The disc is covered with tiny holes called pits. As the disc spins, light is reflected by the shiny disc but not by the pits. Light bouncing off the disc flashes on and off. The player changes these flashes into sound, pictures or computer data.

The PlayStation went on sale at the end of 1994 and was an instant success. A new version, the PlayStation 2, was even more successful. When the PlayStation 4 went on sale in 2013, more than a million were sold on the first day.

Sony's PlayStation was so successful that other electronics companies started making their own games consoles. Microsoft produced the Xbox in 2001 and Nintendo made the Wii in 2006.

TAMAGOTCHI

In the late 1990s, millions of children all over the world were buying electronic pets, also called virtual pets or digital pets. The gadget that set off this craze was the Tamagotchi. It looked like a little plastic egg with a screen.

Pet care

When a Tamagotchi was switched on, an egg appeared on its screen. Then the egg hatched into a small creature, an electronic pet. The pet could be fed and made happy by pressing buttons. The owner could keep the pet happy by playing games with it. It produced droppings (on the screen!), which had to be cleaned up by the owner. As it grew up, it changed from a baby into an older child, then a teenager and finally an adult. If it was ignored or if it wasn't looked after well enough, it could become hungry, sick and even die.

WORLD OF DESIGN

Picking a name

The name of a product is very important. The name often gives buyers an idea of what the product is like or what it does. And it has to be a name that doesn't mean something silly or rude in another language. Tamagotchi comes from two Japanese words – *tamago*, meaning "egg" and *tomodatchi* meaning "friend", so Tamagotchi means "egg-friend".

Tamagotchis were a huge hit. They were sold in Japan first, but a year or so later they were on sale in 30 countries. Their success led to other companies manufacturing their own electronic pets, such as Tiger Electronics' Giga Pets.

More than 80 million Tamagotchis were sold worldwide.

Aki Maita

The Tamagotchi was dreamt up by Aki Maita, who was working for the Japanese toy and video game company, Bandai. In 1990, she joined Bandai's sales and marketing department, where her work involved collecting sales information. Some people might have thought it was a boring job, but not Maita. She said, "it's where I developed an instinct for what will sell and what won't." In Japan, many people live in apartments where pets are not allowed. So, Maita had the idea of making an electronic pet that children could take anywhere with them. It had to be small, portable, able to work anywhere and cute.

Aki Maita invented the Tamagotchi so that all children could have a pet, even if they weren't allowed to keep a real animal.

Human factors

Designers always remember that their products have to be easy for people to use. Buttons, keyboards, screens, hand controllers and other parts have to fit in with the size and shape of people's hands, fingers and bodies. This part of designing products is called human factors or ergonomics.

Market research

An important part of designing any product is market research. It involves asking people what they think about a new product. Maita did market research by asking shoppers in Tokyo what they thought of her ideas for her new electronic pet. Their answers were used to create the Tamagotchi. Maita gave 200 prototypes to schoolgirls to see what they thought. Their comments helped to produce the final design that was manufactured.

There have been nearly 40 different versions of the popular Tamagotchi.

AIBO

Lots of people keep pet dogs for company. Aibo was a pet dog with a difference. He was a **robot**. Aibo stands for **A**rtificial **I**ntelligence ro**BO**t. It also means "pal" or "partner" in Japanese.

Sony spent five years building prototypes, trying out different designs. Aibo was powered by 20 electric motors. He could walk, sit, lie down, move his head, wag his tail and understand up to about 1,000 words spoken to him. He had a camera to see things. He could feel someone stroking him and show when he was happy or angry by flashing green or red lights. He could play with toys, too. Unlike a real dog, Aibo didn't have to be fed or taken for walks, and owners didn't have to clean up any accidental messes!

More than 150,000 Aibos were made between 1999 and 2006.

Prize-winning design

Aibo's body was designed by Japanese artist Hajime Sorayama. It won a string of design awards. Later Aibos had different bodies. One was modelled on a lion cub. Another had a round head that looked like a puppy.

Forty million Furbies were sold all over the world in three years.

FURBIES

In 1998, the year before Aibo went on sale, a strange little electronic pet called a Furby was a must-have toy. A Furby looked like a little owl. It spoke a language called Furbish, but it could learn to speak English. Its mouth, eyes and ears moved. Although Furbies were quite simple toys, they were very, very popular.

IPOD

FAST FACTS

Type of gadget: **Media player**
Produced by: Apple
Introduced in: 2001

The iPod is the world's most popular portable music player. The first iPod played only sound recordings, but later models could do more and more. The latest iPod models can store and play sound, pictures and videos. People used it to store their favourite music, because it was small, beautifully-designed and could store 1,000 songs in a tiny space. Later iPods with bigger memories could store even more songs.

The first Apple iPod changed the way we listen to music while on the move.

32

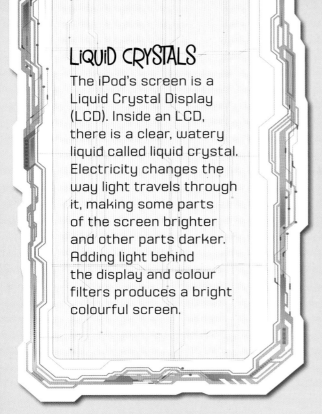

LiQUiD CRYSTALS

The iPod's screen is a Liquid Crystal Display (LCD). Inside an LCD, there is a clear, watery liquid called liquid crystal. Electricity changes the way light travels through it, making some parts of the screen brighter and other parts darker. Adding light behind the display and colour filters produces a bright colourful screen.

Nearly all of the first iPod's switches were replaced by a touch screen.

A better player

The iPod wasn't the first portable music player, but Apple thought the others were badly designed and hard to use, so they tried to make something better. The aim of the design was to make the player easy to use with the smallest number of controls.

The design has changed a lot over the years. The first iPods had press-switches. The latest iPods have a touch screen, much bigger memories and a built-in camera. The iPod has been so popular that more than 350 million of them have been sold all over the world.

ROOMBA

FAST FACTS

Type of gadget: Robot vacuum cleaner
Produced by: iRobot
Introduced in: 2002

In 2002, a new vacuum cleaner went on sale. Called the Roomba, it didn't look much like a vacuum cleaner and it didn't work like other vacuum cleaners. It was a robot. The battery-powered cleaner steered itself around a room, sucking dust up from the floor.

When Roomba was switched on, it followed a cleaning plan stored in its memory. It spiralled around and criss-crossed a room until it thought it had covered the whole floor. If it bumped into something, it reversed, turned and set off in a new direction. Another robot vacuum cleaner called the Trilobite worked differently. It made a map of a room before it started cleaning. Then it used its map to find its way around the room and clean it all. Some of the later models of Roomba can talk. If they get stuck under furniture and can't get free, they can tell someone nearby that they're in trouble and need help.

Since 2002 more than 10 million home robots, including Roomba robot vacuum cleaners, have been sold worldwide.

Kirobo was sent into space to study how astronauts and robots can work together.

SPACE ROBOT

When Japanese astronaut Koichi Wakata arrived at the International Space Station in 2013, a small walking, talking robot called Kirobo was waiting for him. It knew him when it saw him, because the astronaut's face was stored in its memory. It could also understand what Koichi said and spoke back to him.

KINDLE

FAST FACTS

Type of gadget: E-book reader
Produced by: Amazon
Introduced in: 2007

The Kindle is an **e-book** reader designed for the online bookseller Amazon, by a company called Lab126. It stores the text of books in microchips behind its screen. In 2007, the first Kindle could store about 200 books. Since then there have been more Kindles with better screens, bigger memories to hold more books, faster processors and batteries that last longer. Readers don't want the battery to run out just as they get to the best part of a book, so it has to last as long as possible. Some of the latest Kindles have a battery that lasts for up to eight weeks and a memory big enough to store more than 1,000 books.

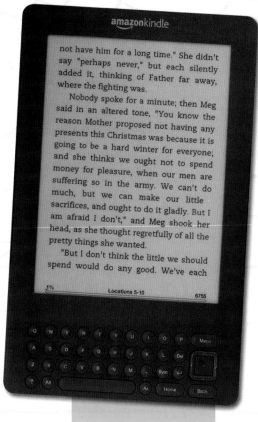

LOOK, NO WIRES!

The Kindle doesn't have to be plugged into a computer to fill its memory with books. It can download (receive) books by radio, by using either **wi-fi** or mobile phone signals. Both of these use radio to send and receive information. This kind of link is called a wireless link.

The first Kindles had a small keyboard built into their case. Later models had a keyboard that appeared on the screen instead.

The Kindle is a computer. It's not like a home computer, which can be programmed to do all sorts of different things. Instead, the Kindle was designed to store books and put their text on its screen. It was designed to be very light, small and portable so that it can be carried easily and used anywhere.

The latest model of the Kindle, the Paperwhite, has a glowing screen that can be read in the dark.

iPhone

The iPhone was such a popular and successful product that by 2014, 500 million iPhones had been sold.

The concept

The iPhone was invented to solve a problem. Apple's iPod had become very popular. Apple were worried that another company might find a way to build something as good as the iPod into a mobile phone. They thought that no one would want to buy iPods any more if that happened.

Apple decided to design its own phone-with-an-iPod first, before someone else did it. In 2005, simple phones just made calls. Phones that had more features were often complicated and hard to use. And they weren't very good at playing music or videos.

Finding the right design

Apple tried lots of different designs, but they weren't happy with any of them until they found the best touch screen they'd ever seen. Most touch screens at that time had to be used with a **stylus** that looked like a little plastic pen. But the new touch screen was much better, because it worked when a fingertip touched it. No stylus was needed. Apple decided to build their phone around the new screen.

The Motorola "brick" was the latest thing in mobile phone technology in the 1980s.

The first mobile phone

The first modern mobile phone was the Motorola DynaTAC. It was so big and heavy that it was nicknamed "the brick". The first mobile phone call was made with a DynaTAC phone in New York City, USA, on 3 April 1973, by Martin Cooper, one of the phone's designers.

Design teams

Apple's design chief, Jonathan Ive, set up a team to design the new phone. It was divided into two smaller teams. One designed the **hardware** and the look of the phone. The other wrote the **software** (the programs) to make the hardware work. The project was top secret, because Apple didn't want anyone to know what they were doing, especially rival companies who might rush their own products into production.

Star parts

Parts that work really well in one product are often used in other products. The touch screen used in the iPhone worked so well that the iPod was redesigned to use it. A bigger version of the screen was also used in the iPad tablet computer.

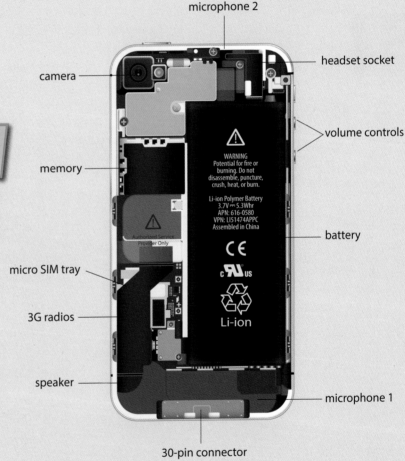

microphone 2

headset socket

camera

volume controls

memory

WARNING
Potential for fire or
burning. Do not
disassemble, puncture,
crush, heat, or burn.

Li-ion Polymer Battery
3.7V ⎓ 5.3Whr
APN: 616-0580
VPN: LIS1474APPC
Assembled in China

Authorized Service
Provider Only

battery

micro SIM tray

3G radios

speaker

microphone 1

Li-ion

30-pin connector

The iPhone is packed with chips, controls, sockets and a large battery.

Refining the design

The design teams built prototypes of the new phone and used them to find out which parts worked well and which parts didn't work as well. They changed and redesigned some parts many times until they were as good as they could be. The result was the iPhone. It went on sale in 2007 and it was an instant hit.

Updating the design

Apple kept improving and redesigning the iPhone. Later models have bigger screens, a bigger memory, a better camera and better software. The phone can sense which way up it's being held and whether it is moving. Some models can even understand what the owner says to it.

The Apple iPad tablet computer uses the same type of touch screen as the iPhone and iPod, only bigger.

THE FUTURE OF ELECTRONIC GADGETS

Since the first electronic gadgets appeared in the 1950s, gadgets have become smaller, they do more, they work better, they work faster and they're more reliable. What will electronic gadgets be like in the future?

In future, the pictures produced by computers, televisions and media players might float in front of you.

Looking into the future

It's very difficult to imagine how things might change in the future. Computers will probably be faster than computers today, so they will be able to do more and do it faster.

There will probably be more robots. Electronic circuits will carry on getting smaller, so the gadgets that use them will be able to do more than they do today. There will be more gadgets that check themselves, looking for faults and telling the owner as soon as something goes wrong, and probably suggesting how to fix it.

More gadgets will be able to connect wirelessly to each other and to the internet, so faster internet connections will be important. And from time to time someone will design a completely new and unexpected gadget, like the tablet computer, that no one knows they need or want until they see it.

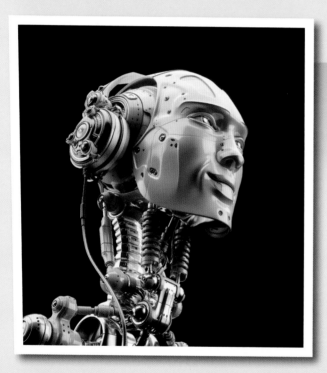

Can you imagine a world where we share our homes and workplaces with robots?

Invent a gadget

Can you think of something you do that a new type of electronic gadget might help you with? Maybe something to do with schoolwork, or playing games, or travelling, or staying healthy? Maybe your gadget could be built into clothes or even injected into someone's body! If so, how would you switch it on and off? Maybe it would have a remote control.

TIMELINE

1904 John Ambrose Fleming invents the diode valve, or tube, marking the beginning of modern electronics

1947 John Bardeen, Walter Brattain and William Shockley invent the transistor

1954 The first transistor radio, the Regency TR-1, goes on sale

1956 Ampex makes the first videotape recorders for television companies

1958 Jack Kilby builds the first **integrated circuit**, or chip

1962 The Telstar communications satellite lets TV viewers see live pictures from the other side of the world for the first time

1971 Ted Hoff invents the microprocessor, the microchip that runs every computer and lots of other electronic gadgets today. The first microprocessor is the Intel 4004. Also, Sony make the first videocassette recorders.

1972 The first video games console, the Magnavox Odyssey designed by Ralph Baer, goes on sale and starts the whole video games industry

1973 In New York City, USA, Martin Cooper makes the first telephone call using a mobile phone

1977 The Commodore PET, the first all-in-one personal computer, goes on sale. Also, the Apple II designed by Steve Wozniak, becomes the first successful mass-produced personal computer.

1979 The Sony Walkman becomes the first successful personal stereo

1981 IBM launches the IBM Personal Computer, the ancestor of all PCs today

1994 Sony introduces the PlayStation video games console

2007 The first Apple iPhone and Amazon Kindle e-book reader go on sale

2013 Kirobo becomes the first walking, talking robot in space when he is sent to work on board the International Space Station with Japanese astronaut Koichi Wakata

GLOSSARY

analogue type of device that carries or stores information in a continuously variable form. Old-fashioned vinyl discs and tape recorders were analogue devices.

cassette case containing a length of magnetic tape for recording sound or pictures

CD compact disc, a flat, shiny disc used for storing music, text or pictures, in the form of a digital code that is read by shining light on the disc

chip short for microchip, a tiny electronic part containing one or more circuits, used in mobile phones, computers and other electronic gadgets

computer program set of instructions followed by a computer

console box or case with controls. A games console is a box that controls a video game or games played using a television set.

data factual information, especially information processed and stored by a computer or another electronic device

digital type of device that carries or stores information in the form of a code representing numbers. Computers and mobile phones are digital devices.

e-book electronic version of a book, stored in a digital form in a computer, e-book reader, smartphone or other electronic device

electric circuit path an electric current flows along. The current flows from a battery, or another power source, around the circuit and back to the battery.

electronic using devices, circuits or methods that work by controlling particles called electrons

floppy disk small magnetic disc that was used in the past for storing computer data

graphic drawing or illustration

hard disk rigid magnetic disc, often inside a computer, for storing computer programs and data

hardware parts of a computer or other electronic equipment that you can see and touch (compare this to software)

integrated circuit tiny electronic circuit inside a microchip

magnetic tape long, thin ribbon of plastic covered with magnetic particles, for recording music, pictures or other information

manufacturer company that makes products with the help of chemical processes and machines

mass-produced made in large numbers in factories

media player device or computer program for storing and playing music, pictures or videos

optical to do with light

personal computer small computer designed to be used by one person

personal stereo small portable device for playing music recorded on a tape cassette, CD or digitally

prototype first version of a design, which is then copied and improved upon

robot mechanical device programmed to do work normally done by a person. Some robots look like mechanical people, but others look like mechanical arms or other machines.

satellite device or machine that orbits a planet or moon

software programs and applications run by a computer, smartphone or other electronic equipment (compare this to hardware)

stylus tool like a pen used to operate early touch screens

transistor device for amplifying electronic signals (making them bigger) or switching them on and off. The microchips inside electronic devices, including computers and mobile phones, contain thousands, or millions, of transistors.

valve early electronic device for controlling the flow of electrons around a circuit. Known as a tube, or vacuum tube, in the United States.

wi-fi method for connecting computers, mobile phones and other electronic gadgets to each other or to the internet by using radio signals

FIND OUT MORE

Books

Computer Games Designer, Mark Featherstone (Raintree, 2014)

Gadgets, Games, Robots and the Digital World (Dorling Kindersley, 2011)

How Cool Stuff Works, Chris Woodford (Dorling Kindersley, 2008)

Robots, Chips and Techno-stuff, Glenn Murphy (Macmillan Children's Books, 2011)

The Big Book of Electronic Adventures, Carmen Scupin (Franzis Verlag, 2013)

Websites

transition.fcc.gov/cgb/kidszone/history_cellphone.html
Find out about the history of mobile phones from the Federal Communications Commission in the United States.

www.labnol.org/gadgets/electronic-gadgets-timeline/12391
You'll find a timeline of cool gadgets from the 1970s to the present day.

www.madlab.org/electrnx/electrnx.html
This website offers a beginner's guide to electronics.

www.pcworld.com/article/123950/the_50_greatest_gadgets_of_the_past_50_years
This website includes a list of the 50 greatest gadgets of the past 50 years with links to more pages about their history and technology.

Places to visit

The Science Museum
Exhibition Road, South Kensington
London SW7 2DD
Tel: 020 7942 4000
Email: info@sciencemuseum.ac.uk
Website: www.sciencemuseum.org.uk

A world-class museum containing
thousands of exhibits tracing the
history of science and technology,
including computers, radio, telephone
technology, sound recording and the
internet.

The Mansion
Bletchley Park, Sherwood Drive
Bletchley, Milton Keynes MK3 6EB
Tel: 01908 640404
Email: contact form on website
Website: www.bletchleypark.org.uk

Bletchley Park is the top-secret
establishment where German codes
were broken during World War II,
allowing Britain to read coded German
military messages. The world's first
programmable electronic computer,
called Colossus, was built at Bletchley
Park to help break enemy codes faster.

Ideas for research

The world's most powerful computers are called supercomputers. They work
faster than other computers. They are used to do work that needs a huge
number of calculations to be done very quickly. Can you find out who uses
supercomputers and what they do? Here's a clue – what will the weather be like
tomorrow?

Thousands of pet dogs, cats and other animals have microchips inside their
bodies. The chips were put there by vets. Why do you think this was done? Do you
think people should be microchipped?

More than 10 million home robots have been sold all over the world. If you could
have your own robot at home, what would you use it for? Can you find out if a
robot has already been made to do this sort of job?

INDEX